POWER
of
SOLUTION

POWER
O*f*
SOLUTION

GOD'S FINAL ORDER AGAINST YOUR
STUBBORN PROBLEMS

LIZZY IWEALA, PH.D.

authorHOUSE®

AuthorHouse™
1663 Liberty Drive
Bloomington, IN 47403
www.authorhouse.com
Phone: 1-800-839-8640

Published by AuthorHouse   11/14/2012

ISBN: 978-1-4772-9175-7 (sc)
ISBN: 978-1-4772-9174-0 (e)

Library of Congress Control Number: 2012921608

Any people depicted in stock imagery provided by Thinkstock are models, and such images are being used for illustrative purposes only.
Certain stock imagery © Thinkstock.

This book is printed on acid-free paper.

DEDICATION

This book is dedicated, first, to my greatest Teacher, the Holy Spirit Himself; and second, to all the global radical intercessors for Jesus who have refused to become failures in the school of prayer.

Appreciation

My sincere appreciation goes to all the intercessors in my life and ministry. Special thanks to all my spiritual confidants whose positive affirmations to the call of God upon my life stands as a constant reminder of His faithfulness.

CONTENTS

INTRODUCTION

When you become tired of the continual bombardments of the enemy upon your life, know that it is time to cry out to the Power of Solutions—God Himself—to declare the final order against the evil harassment of the enemy on your life.

The ability to maintain a holy, aggressive, and defensive position when utilizing these effective prayer strategies is the key to causing commotion and havoc in the camp of your enemy. This book will teach you some of the divine techniques on how to tap into the divine socket of the Power of Solutions to download your breakthroughs.

Some of the prayer declarations in this book will help mandate your unprecedented victory over your stubborn problems.

Therefore put on your spiritual armor as you embark on this radical spiritual warfare. This is your divine opportunity to declare to your enemy that "enough is enough" in the MIGHTY NAME Jesus.

POWER OF SOLUTIONS

Power of Solutions is the Power above all powers capable of mandating solutions to the stubborn problems in your life. The Almighty Jehovah is the Power of Solutions. The good news is that believers can now plug themselves into the socket of the Power of Solutions through the blood and the name of our Lord and Savior Jesus Christ. Once they do this, they will see their problems turn around for good to the glory and praise of His holy name.

The unfortunate truth is that many people today are suffering in the hands of the enemy because of lack of knowledge. The Bible declares in Hosea 4:6 that "my people are destroyed for lack of knowledge. Because you have rejected knowledge, I also will reject you from being priest for me." People don't realize the authority they have over the enemy through the name of Jesus, and some of those who are aware of such authority sometimes fail to utilize it by allowing the enemy to take them for a ride.

Unfortunately, most people dabble into various diabolic powers in order to obtain solutions to their problems and, in so doing so, inherit more demons into their lives resulting in increased problems. The solutions that diabolic mediums provide are usually short-lived, but their destructive consequences are long-lasting. Why? This is very simple to explain.

The gifts of such powers are usually likened to that of a "trade by barter." What is trade by barter? It is a process where goods and services are exchanged for the benefit of each other. For example, someone who has a bag of baking flour can exchange it with me for a gallon of milk. In the same manner, when a person visits diabolic powers to seek solutions to a problem, the demons respond to the request of their victim (client) by creating a temporary or *pseudo* solution. In return, they demand an exchange from their client, which becomes an evil legal-standing order for a stronghold in the life of its victim. Take, for example, a woman who brings her sick baby to a shaman (occult priest) or a witch doctor for healing. Unknown to her, the priest or doctor creates a marriage covenant with evil powers on behalf of the child. Several years go by and the daughter is now of age to get married but, to her amazement, no one is proposing to her. Evil powers are contending against her suitors. These powers are jealously wicked; it will take aggressive prayer declarations and the mercy of God to break such evil covenants. That's why you have to be spiritually alert to who lays hands on you or your kids.

Evil manipulators can even exchange a child's destiny. You might have seen a smart and intelligent boy suddenly become very dull and slow with his academic work and you wonder what is going on with him. Well, the child could be suffering from the powers that have access to him through an evil altar—an open gateway to the spirit world. That's why you have to pray with holy aggression, reverse every evil work over the life of your dear one, and close that gate.

If you find yourself suffering from the effect of an evil power, I advise you to trigger a holy anger within your spirit through effective prayer declarations in order to penetrate the camp of the enemy and recover everything he has stolen from you. The Bible declares that "from the days of John the Baptist until now the kingdom of heaven suffers violence and the violent take it by force" (Matthew 11:12). Therefore, you will have to pursue, overtake, and recover—with spiritual force all that the enemy has stolen from you. Yes! You have to recover your marriage, your sons and daughters, your peace, your joy, your prayer life, your health, your ministry, and your blessings. Do not make the great mistake of asking the devil to relinquish that which is rightly yours by the virtue of the finished work of the Cross. Just go into his camp and snatch it by force. You have the divine authority to recover all of your stolen goods and, at the same time, reclaim your destiny in the name of Jesus.

Sometimes you will find beautiful ladies and handsome men who are gracefully aging alone because their attempts to maintain a relationship that could develop into a marital union have always proven futile. So no one has ever asked for their hand in marriage. Why? The problem could be due to an evil, spiritual covenant, or a spirit husband or wife warring against their social breakthroughs. If this applies to your situation or someone close to you, I encourage you to pray effectively and strategically against those forces that persistently contend against breakthrough.

Pray with holy aggression the following prayer declarations:

Prayer Declarations

1. Power of Solutions: arise and manifest your power in my life. I pray.

2. Powers contending against my breakthrough, collide with the Rock of Ages—Jesus Himself.

3. Demons from hell, I command you to be roasted by fire in the name of Jesus.

4. I refuse to be ignorant of my spiritual potential, in the name of Jesus.

5. I am exalted high above all my problems because I have the Power of Solutions working in my favor, in the name of Jesus.

Evil legal-Standing Order

A legal-standing order is an order established by an authority concerning a particular issue. For example, a traffic sign with a speed limit of 30 mph at a specific road or location stands as a legal-standing order that motorists must abide by. A ruling by a court judge is a legal-standing order. A written agreement to buy a house or a verbal agreement to fix a leaky roof in exchange for compensation is also considered a legal-standing order that binds each party to the agreement. With God, the legal-standing order between a believer and God is the blood of Jesus. The blood of Jesus was paid as a ransom for our sins; therefore, we have been reconciled to the Father by the virtue of that shed blood. And, in so doing, we can boldly connect to the heavenly Power of Solutions for our breakthroughs in the name of Jesus. So, our prayers avail by the legal-standing order of the blood and the name of Jesus.

An evil legal-standing order is, therefore, made possible through an evil covenant, which could be made willfully or out of ignorance.

It could be made by an individual or by a third party through a voluntary or involuntary action. Most often, people who decide to initiate themselves in witchcraft practices or occultism must abide by the rules or principles that guide such practices. However, when a member decides to act against such rules, he or she is confronted with or judged by the standing order. In the same manner, when a child is being initiated to an evil spirit and a marriage covenant is established, an evil legal-standing order will also be established to substantiate that covenant. Then, many years later, the child grows into an adult and realizes that she has been unable to maintain a steady relationship with the opposite sex. Everybody is wondering why she is not yet married. Sometimes, she has a boyfriend, but once the issue of marriage is raised, the boyfriend suddenly retreats out of the picture. Have you ever wondered why? Perhaps during her childhood, her parents took her to a shaman or witch doctor due to one ailment or the other. The parents were looking for solutions to their child's predicament, unfortunately, in all the wrong places. So now, upon talk of marriage, the evil legal order takes effect to resist the marriage. Even if the woman has become a born-again child of God, that covenant must be renounced and broken in the name of Jesus. This is why, if a permanent breakthrough is going to occur, most often, some kind of spiritual mapping is needed in order to get to the foundation of the problem. Spiritual mapping is a means of collecting relevant, foundational information that could identify the root of stubborn problems. It is paramount to deal with stubborn problems from the root. Jesus said in Matthew 15:13: "Every plant which My heavenly Father has not planted will be uprooted." A total victory is inevitable when a problem is dealt with at its foundation.

Evil legal orders can also kick in against someone through an open door by the virtue of having things that belongs to the devil.

I went to a party once where a friend said, "Oh! Lizzy, try this." She pointed to the Devil's Egg.

"No thanks!" I replied. I was not going to mess with any devil's food.

She said that I was being superstitious. "It's just a name," she added.

"Yes, agreed. It's just a name," I said, "but one thing's sure, I'm not going to mess with any kind of devil's food, especially when it's clearly labeled the devil's egg." It would take putting me under some kind of sedation in order to force feed me with such a demonic-named food, as I call it from the spiritual point of view.

The Bible has warned to flee from any appearance of sin and my desire is to obey but, in the name of fashion, I see kids wearing tee-shirts with skulls and evil symbols. Who knows why some kids act so crazy and deadly? Parents should be very careful of what they buy for their kids. Those lines of clothing would go out of business if they counted on me as their client because I will not buy from them. People also wear all sorts of jewelry with demonic symbols, in the name of fashion. They end up in bondage, having terrible nightmares of unknown origin. Some even lose their minds as a result of such possessions. When these people go to their physicians for a solution, they often label the disturbed person as being psychotic.

Instead of concerning themselves with such a diagnosis, they should throw away all evil clothing, jewelry, and other evil things from their possession and make this prayer declaration with holy aggression: "Any evil altar or voice challenging my liberty in Christ Jesus, you are a liar in the name of Jesus. I silence you forever."

Believers are to be spiritually alert at all times since the devil is busy and is coming up with all kinds of gimmicks to lure people into complacency, spiritual blindness, and bondage. Therefore, we must be vigilant not to fall prey into the wicked hands of the devil.

This reminds me of the story of a little, wise bird who decided to stay in flight mode. The entire community of birds got to talking about him; it became a regular part of their little gossip community. Finally, the elder birds decided to inquire of this new venture of his and were shocked by his response. The bird responded saying, "I have realized that man has learned to shoot without missing; therefore, I have also decided to fly without perching."

We can learn from that little bird by realizing that the enemy is very busy walking to and fro, looking for someone to devour; therefore, we should also embark on praying without ceasing, on meditating on the word of the Lord—the Bible—the Sword of the Spirit.

It is very important to position yourself for breakthrough. You must refuse to compromise your God-given authority. You are a man of valor. You are a daughter of Zion, therefore, stooping to anything less than that is not acceptable in the sight of the Lord. God frowns when we shortchange our divine privileges, and it is an abomination to do so. It is also an absolute disgrace when a prince takes a role reversal with his father's servant. Let's see what the book of Ecclesiastes 10:7 says, "I have seen servants on horses while princes walk on the ground like servants." You know that something is definitely wrong with this picture; it's an absolute, natural error. The Scripture is saying that believers are not tapping into the Power of Solutions. Lack of spiritual knowledge has actually placed most believers into what I call "spiritual prison." This lazy attitude among believers has resulted in a larger number of spiritual casualties because if you live in servant hood to the enemy, he will take the upper hand over your life. You cannot afford to let down your guard at any point in time. The enemy is tossing some of God's people around like a football because they have become powerless Christians as a result of self-satisfaction, prayerlessness, and compromise—all of which have so dangerously invaded the core of the Christian church.

The church must rise up to her challenges by getting connected to the divine Power of Solutions which is God Himself through the name of Jesus. We need the Power of Solutions in every department of our lives. We need the Power of Solutions in order to cause commotion in the camp of our enemy. We need the Power of Solutions to break strongholds in our foundation. We need the Power of Solutions for unprecedented breakthrough in our lives that would mandate a "come and see miracle." When you get connected to the Power of Solutions, and you pray in the name of Jesus, the heavens will hear your cry, and your breakthrough has no choice but to manifest speedily in your life.

You must put on the whole armor of God and get ready for battle. You are about to engage in some strategic prayer declarations that will release your breakthrough because you have made a conscious decision to say, "Enough is enough of the enemy's foolishness in my life." You are by faith connected to the Power of solutions—God Himself—the Court of Heaven is ready to rule in your favor.

Before embarking on any spiritual engagement or warfare, first do the following:

1. Thank God for being God in your life.
2. Appreciate Him for releasing His Son Jesus from heaven to come and die for your sins.

3. Confess any sin of omission or commission that might stand against your breakthrough.

4. Plead the blood of Jesus over your loved ones and upon your life and as covering against any wicked arrow from the camp of your enemy.

5. Declare words boldly as you exercise your spiritual authority over the enemy.

6. Pursue, overtake, and recover by force everything the enemy has stolen from you.

7. Give the enemy a marching order to where you want him to go or what you want to become of him in the name of Jesus.

8. With the blood of Jesus, cover your recovered blessings, family members, health, marriage, children, ministry, finances, and everything that has been recovered, including yourself.

9. Praise the Lord and dance unto him like David did when the Lord gave him victory over his enemies, in the name of Jesus.

Power of Solutions against the "Almost-There Syndrome"

The "Almost-There Syndrome" is also known as "failure at the edge of a breakthrough." This is when success slips out of your hands without any struggle. Some call it the "Spirit of Pisgah." This refers to when Moses was so close to the Promised Land, but he was not permitted to set his feet on it. He could only view the land from Mt. Pisgah, which became the wall that separated him from his Promised Land.

Esau's life was the epitome of an almost-there syndrome. He allowed his birthright to slip out of his hands for the sake of a bowl of porridge. When food becomes a curse in one's life, it is a thing of sorrow and shame. It was for Esau, but he was able to almost recover that which was lost in his life. He desperately went out to hunt so he could make stew for his aging father, Isaac, who was ready and willing to unleash uncommon blessings into his life after eating the stew. However, that was not meant to be because by the time he returned from his hunting trip, his brother, Jacob, with his mother as his accomplice usurped the blessing that was meant for Esau.

Esau, coming to the knowledge of this, cried out in agony to his father asking him to bless him. For such reason, Isaac proclaimed some blessings upon the life of Esau, and that blessing was able to break the yoke of the almost-there syndrome in his life. Thanks be to God Almighty who is our Father of second chances.

This is the yoke-breaking proclamation by Isaac to Esau, according to Genesis 27:38-40 as he cries out to his father to bless him: "And Esau said to his father, 'Have you only one blessing, my father? Bless me—me also, O my father!' And Esau lifted up his voice and wept. Then Isaac, his father, answered and said to him: 'Behold, your dwelling shall be of the fatness of the earth, and of the dew of heaven from above. By your sword you shall live, and you shall serve your brother; and it shall come to pass, when you become restless, that you shall break his yoke from your neck.'"

God is saying that when you become restless of experiencing failures in your life, then it is time for you to rise up and break that yoke through the divine Power of Solution. Break the yoke of "que sera sera" mentality. Reject the spirit of failure and rise up as a daughter of Zion and the man of valor of which you are by the special grace of God, and walk valiantly into the camp of the enemy. Recover by force your success that has been tied up and laying waste in the camp of the enemy due to sheer wickedness. Isaiah 10:27 says, "It shall come to pass in that day that his burden will be taken away from your shoulder, and his yoke from your neck, and the yoke will be destroyed because of the anointing oil."

Break the evil cycle of failure in your life in the name of Jesus and maintain your victory, which is rightfully yours through the justified work of the Cross. That is why you must feed your faith and starve the power of doubt and failure in your life. I mean that you should starve the spirit of doubt and failure to death because when you starve something for a long time, whether man or plant, death is inevitable. Therefore, feed your faith and starve your doubt. God has a better plan for your life. *"For I know the thoughts that I think toward of you, says the Lord, thoughts of peace and not of evil, to give you a future and a hope" (Jeremiah 29:11).*

I encourage you to rise up and walk above the failure mentality as you make the following prayer declarations that will help mandate your divine success through the Power of Solutions in the name of Jesus.

Prayer Declarations

1. In the name of Jesus, I break the yoke of "near-success syndrome."
2. Power of Solutions, manifest your depth in my life, I pray.
3. I reject the yoke of failure in my life, in the mighty name of Jesus.
4. My foundation, vomit any seed of failure in my life, in the name of Jesus.
5. My life, you will not rotate in a cycle of failure, in the name of Jesus.
6. Failure at the edge of my breakthrough—you must die, in the name of Jesus.
7. I have the grace of God to succeed, in the name of Jesus.
8. Anointing to succeed manifest in my life, in the mighty name of Jesus.

9. I will not eat the bread of failure, in the mighty name of Jesus.

10. Power of Solutions, break every yoke of limitation in my life. I pray this in the name of Jesus.

11. Fire of God, penetrate my life and consume all powers, inducing failure in my life. In the name of Jesus, I pray.

Power of Solutions against Infirmities

Isaiah 53:5—"He was wounded for our transgressions, He was bruised for our iniquities. The chastisement for our peace was upon Him, and by His stripes we are healed."

Psalm 103:1-3—"Bless the LORD, O my soul, and all that is within me, bless His holy name! Bless the LORD, O my soul, and forget not all His benefits: Who forgives all your iniquities, and who heals all thy diseases."

Jeremiah 8:22—"Is there no balm in Gilead, Is there no physician there? Why then is there no recovery for the health of the daughters of my people?

Matthew 15:13—"Every plant which My heavenly Father has not planted will be uprooted."

Healing is one of the benefits of a believer. When you receive Christ as your personal Savior, you are automatically enrolled in His benefit plan of Salvation. It is now your divine right to tap into His divine resources, and claim that which is now yours by the virtue of His shed blood at Calvary.

Some schools of thought believe that divine healing is of the old and no longer has any ground in today's Christianity. I strongly believe that it is one of the devil's gimmicks in keeping God's people in bondage. I can boldly speak of the divine truth of God's healing power still in effect from a very personal perspective; therefore, no one can talk me out of this truth. I have experienced God's physical, healing power in my life and the saying "experience is the best teacher" speaks for itself. God is still in the healing business. You must not allow the enemy to rob you of this fact.

I have seen patients who have been written off by medical authorities, so their family members stand in the gap, interceding in prayer, trusting God to His Word, hoping for a miracle. God, hearing their cry and seeing their faith, stepped in from heaven above and turned a hopeless situation hopeful. It is equally true to know that God does heal through medical science. God has given man increased wisdom in all areas of life, and the invention of more sophisticated medical equipment and new treatment regimes can be associated with such truth.

I remember going with one of my friends and prayer partners to visit one of our new Christian converts. She had confided in us about her upcoming surgical plan. Her doctor had found a cyst in one of her organs and surgery was recommended. We prayed for her, and during the prayer session something extraordinary occurred. While we were praying for her, she fell down and started to roll on the floor. Rolling on the floor is a common occurrence during a deliverance process; therefore, we continued our praying process and followed by a praise song. By the time we finished praying, the sister was just looking at us in awe of what had happed. She said she saw herself tied from the neck to the legs. As we continued praying, someone came and was unraveling the rope, and she was set free. We praised God for such a revelation and deliverance.

The following week, the sister went in for her surgery. After she woke up from the anesthesia, the surgeon came to her room to give his post-operative report to her and her husband. In his hand was a copy of the x-ray. The surgeon was a little hesitant to speak at first but finally told them his observations. He pointed on the x-ray to the very spot where the cyst was. He said that to his amazement, when they opened her up, the cyst was no longer there. It was gone. She used the opportunity to tell the doctor about her experience during our prayer session with her. She said she strongly believed that during that prayer session, God Himself reached down to her and performed His divine surgical procedure on her. There are certain divine interventions that will defy medical explanation, and this story is one of them. God is still in the healing process. Do not allow anyone to talk you out of it.

One day I was talking to a Muslim doctor who said he had been so sick the past weekend with a cold and a stuffy nose. I asked him if he was still feeling stuffy, and he said yes. He sounded real sick, indeed. I asked him if he wouldn't mind my praying for him, and He said, "No, with all pleasure." This doctor had known that I am a Christian, and he is very cognizant of my uncompromised stand when it comes to publicly espousing my faith. I reached out my right hand, touched his nose, and said a simple prayer: "In the name of Jesus, I command this stuffiness to leave." He was instantly healed. He went around telling everybody about what he had just experienced. He told them that I had healed him, but I was quick to correct him, saying that I did not heal him but that God did it through me and that I am very grateful to God for His mercies.

A few days later, the same doctor took me to one of his patients and asked me to pray for her and I did. Two weeks later, he handed me a note requesting that I pray for his family and marriage. This very doctor, though a Muslim, had personally experienced God's divine touch and decided to embrace the truth of God through his continuous praying with me. When you have a personal experience of the Almighty touch of GOD, absolutely nobody can take away the truth that God is still in His healing business because He is the Power of Solutions.

The Bible declares that God performed various kinds of miracles in Egypt. Christ came and also healed all manner of sicknesses and infirmities. The dead were raised from sleep, the blind received their sight, the crippled walked, the deaf received their hearing, and the insane became sane. If Christ is the same yesterday, today, and will be the same tomorrow, then rest assured that healing is still the same today. Therefore, there is balm in Gilead, and the daughters and sons of God must be healed by the mercy and grace of God.

Take the above healing Scriptures as your divine prescription and meditate on them daily. God will always respond to His word. Healing belongs to us. The stripes that Christ received on his body were not in vain; they were for our healing. Therefore, by His stripes we are healed. Healing is ours for keeps. It is for the believers' benefit; therefore, you must refuse to be short-changed by claiming your divine healing in the name of Jesus.

If you have been afflicted by any form of sickness, I wish to encourage you to embark on a positive confession of your healing. Search the Bible and write down as many healing Scripture verses as you can find, and confess them as many times as possible in a day. There is power in spoken words. Declare in the name of Jesus that you are going to live and not die. You can meditate on some of the above Scriptures. Jesus is the same yesterday, today, and forever and still performing miracles indeed. At the name of Jesus all manners of afflictions must bow. Every seed of affliction inside of you must be uprooted because the Lord has said so. "Every plant which My heavenly Father has not planted will be uprooted" (Matthew 15:13). Your body is the temple of God therefore any form of affliction dwelling inside of you is a trespasser and guilty as charged. I declare the effect of the Power of Solutions against any affliction warring against your member in the Mighty name of Jesus.

Do not allow the lies of the enemy that you cannot be healed because you are a sinner or that you deserved to be afflicted due to a repercussion of a past action of yours. The devil has always been a liar. The very moment you receive Christ as your personal Savior, your sins are forgiven and the benefit of that confession, which includes healing, becomes rightfully yours. David was cognizant of this fact when he wrote in Psalm 103:1-4:

"Bless the Lord, O my soul and forget not all His benefits:
Who forgives all your iniquities, who heals all your diseases,
Who redeems your life from destruction,
Who crowns you with loving kindness and tender mercies."

God desires that His children live in perfect health. The stripes that Christ received on His body took care of the issues of afflictions and diseases. Therefore, by those stripes you are healed, Glory be to the name of the Lord. Do not rely on how you feel. I encourage you to depend on the word of God and confess it on a daily basis.

Make the following prayer declarations with holy anger. Permit your spirit-man to provoke holy aggression to rise up in you as you make these declarations against the powers of affliction trying to terminate your life before its time. The devil is a thief and all he wants to do is to steal, to kill, and to destroy just as indicated in the Bible. But God Himself has come to give you life abundantly. Halleluiah to the Lord!

Prayer declarations

1. I confess that by His stripes I am healed; therefore, any power of affliction in my body must die, in the name of Jesus.
2. I stand by the authority and the benefits of my salvation through Christ Jesus; therefore, powers of affliction over my health hear the word of the Lord and afflict yourselves in the name of Jesus.
3. I command any affliction in my body to jump out and afflict its sender, in the name of Jesus.
4. I shall not die but live and declare the works of the Lord; therefore, your affliction you will not kill me. I command you to turn around and afflict your sender, in the name of Jesus.
5. I receive the divine balm of Gilead prescribed by the Great Physician, in the name of Jesus.
6. Yoke of affliction, break your hold upon my health and die, in the name of Jesus.
7. In the name of Jesus, I shut every door of affliction into my life.
8. I uproot every seed of affliction planted in my life, in the name of Jesus.
9. Yokes of cancer, hypertension, diabetes, lupus, kidney failure, liver failure, AIDS, anemia, blood diseases, asthma,

blindness, respiratory failure, break your hold! In the name of Jesus, I pray.

10. By the authority in the word of God, I declare myself untouchable, unreachable, and invisible to the powers affliction.

11. By the very power in the word of God, I claim divine immunity over the powers of afflictions and diverse categories of afflictions.

12. Power of Solutions in the name of Jesus, by the Power that makes you God, manifest your Power in my situation. I pray. Amen.

13. Thank you Lord for the power of healing that flows through Emmanuel's vein and is now flowing into my vein. By His stripes I claim my divine health, in the name of Jesus.

14. I will not drink from the cup of affliction, in the name of Jesus.

15. I will not eat the bread of affliction, in the name of Jesus I pray.

16. Owner of evil baggage of afflictions, carry your load. In the mighty name of Jesus.

17. I swim in the cleansing and healing river of the blood of Jesus, I pray. Amen.

Power of Solutions against Dream Killers

Dream killers are made up of both internal and external factors. It is always good to identify the factor that is working against your destiny. Here are some signs to alert you when a dream killer is in the camp:

- You had a great dream that died when you woke up the next morning.
- You had a great idea that ended up on a piece of paper or in a document on your laptop.
- You started a project and the zeal died along the way. The project remains unfinished.
- You told a colleague or friend your fabulous ideas. He gave you all the reasons why your idea is not workable, and you believed him and allowed the dream to die.

If any of the above applies to you, then it is likely that you are suffering under the influence of physical or spiritual dream killers. Therefore, you must pray with holy aggression in order to break the influence of such killer over your life. You are more than a conqueror. You are on the winning side, and the winning side is with Jesus.

There are spiritual and physical dream killers. Both categories of dream killers are equally dangerous. The only difference between the two is their nature. The spiritual dreams killers are invisible to the naked eyes whereas the physical ones are visible.

What are the objectives of the dream killers? Their main objective is to subject their victims to perpetual failure. They are destiny killers; they will make sure that their victims embrace only the glory of the valley. Whenever a victim makes any effort to climb out of their valley situation, spiritual dream killers get real upset and even endeavor to chain their victim to the root of the valley. That is why you need discernment to the root of the problem and effective prayer to break loose from such yokes. Sometimes fasting and prayer is a mandate.

However, physical dream killers are people such as the sons of Jacob who after listening to Joseph narrate his dreams on how their sheaves had to bow down to his sheaf; how the sun, moon, and the eleven stars bowed down to him also, sought for a way to terminate Joseph's life rather than witness the manifestation of his dream. They even called him "the dreamer." A comprehensive report of the story of Joseph's dream is in the book of Genesis chapter 37. I encourage you to read that chapter as it will surely captivate your interest while you obtain a firsthand account of this biblical event.

Another category of physical dream killers is those who are cognizant of your potential but out of jealousy will discourage you from attaining your greater heights. They are usually your close friends and associates, sometimes relatives who I describe as "evil attachments." They are your enemies of progress. They are good in withholding vital information that could propel you to your breakthrough. They are already failures and knowing that you will succeed with any amount of information given to you, they would rather throw such information away than let you have it.

You do not need dream killers around you because they are dangerously wicked. Instead of seeing you succeed in life, they'd rather choke life out of you before your time. The goal of Joseph's brothers was to terminate his life; but for the divine will of God, their plan did not succeed. Instead, it became the vehicle that propelled Joseph to the manifestation of his dream—his destiny—as he was escorted to Egypt through God's divine ordinances.

Spiritual dream killers are evil remote controls and microphones who listen to your conversations and relay them to their evil master so they can brainstorm a way to abort your dream. That is why you have to exercise wisdom in what you disclose to others. Sometimes it is wise to realize a dream before sharing the information to others because if you share your ideas or plans to a dream killer, it is likely that they will look for avenues to destroy them. They work with familiar spirits to monitor your moves and agenda.

The spiritual strongman or stronghold usually originates from the father's house of the victim. Evil powers of a mother's house cannot be excluded either. For example, there are some young men suffering from the powers of perpetual failure because the root of their problems are linked to either their paternal or maternal root. That is why you have to come against evil powers of your parent's house in the name of Jesus.

Protect your dream with fasting and prayer. Birth your dream through positive affirmation. There is power in spoken words. God wants you to speak out your desire, and he will honor it. Speak life. Speak blessings upon your life, upon the lives of your children, and see them come to pass. Job 22:28 says, "You will also declare a thing and it will be established for you. So light will shine on your ways." Therefore, declare life and not death.

Act your dream through the work of faith action by walking toward it. For example, if your dream is to become a lawyer, first, you will have to make inquiries as to the courses that are required for such profession. Second, you will have to enroll in a school in order to take the relevant courses. The process of going to a school and enrolling into a class is an act of faith toward your dream of becoming a lawyer. Therefore, works must accompany faith. Attach yourself with positively-minded people and enablers and avoid the opposite. Unfortunately, dream killers most often are the very individuals who are closest to you. They are the ones you sometimes draw closer to as your confidants; however, their bites are similar to that of a rat that fans and bites its victims at the same time. You must be very vigilant and spiritually alert when in close proximity with dream killers.

The good news is that our God Almighty is the Power of Solutions against your dream killers. The yoke of the dream killers must be destroyed in the name of Jesus. Dream killers are witches and wizards, and they are wickedly wicked. The Bible clearly states in Exodus 22:18: "You shall not permit a sorceress [witch] to live.' The goal of a witch is always to suck life out of her victim. Therefore, do not permit them to live—kill them with your strategic prayer declarations in the authority and the name of Jesus.

You are going to pray now with holy aggression, and kill all the dream killers assigned against your destiny before they get hold of you. Therefore, in the name of Jesus, stop them before they stop you.

Prayer declarations

1. Power of Solutions! Manifest in my life and destroy the dream killers of my life, in the name of Jesus.

2. Any power assigned to kill my dream, you are a liar. In the name of Jesus, destroy yourself.

3. Like unto the order of Joseph, evil powers of my father's house, expose yourselves and be disgraced in the name of Jesus.

4. Any power withholding information to my greatness, release it now to me in the name of Jesus and die.

5. Evil attachment to my life, in the name of Jesus, detach yourself and catch fire.

6. Spiders of my dream, die in the name of Jesus.

7. Cobwebs of stagnation hovering around my dream to frustrate it, catch fire in the name of Jesus.

8. Spiritual strongman assigned to relay my progress to my enemy, be bound in the name of Jesus.

9. Evil remote control assigned to remote control my progress, fall down and crash in the name of Jesus.

10. In the name of Jesus, I silence every evil voice making enchantment and divination against my dream.

11. In the mighty name of Jesus, I must dream big by the grace and mercy of God.

12. My God-given dream, hear the word of God, and thrive in the mighty name of Jesus.

13. You dream killer, in the name of Jesus, I command you to choke yourself to death.

14. You dream killer of my life, in the name of Jesus, dig your own grave and bury yourself.

15. My dreams to success, hear the word of the LORD, and come alive in the name of Jesus.

16. Power of Solutions, by the power that makes you God, manifest in my dream life and turn my situation around for good, I pray.

17. Any power assigned to abort my destiny, die in the name of Jesus.

18. Uncommon anointing to make my dream come alive, fall upon me in the name of Jesus. I pray. Amen.

POWER OF SOLUTIONS AGAINST MARRIAGE BREAKERS

So then, they are no longer two but one flesh.
Therefore what God has joined together, let not man
separate.
—Matthew 19:6

The institution of marriage is under a very serious attack from the camp of the enemy. God cherishes the institution of marriage to the extent that He gave a divine commandment as per evidence of the above Scripture. A song writer penned: "A family that prays together stays together." Prayer is a much-attacked affair. The enemy knows that if you can only pray, your trouble will have to subject itself to God's authority and your problem is sure to receive divine solution. Therefore, the devil in his beguiling nature fires arrows of diverse distractions in order to render his victims physically and spiritually handicapped in the area of prayer. The good news is that you have the power to resist him in the name of Jesus by obstructing his entrance into your home, by showing him the red flag, which is the blood of Jesus.

You must learn to pray in and out of season. You must pray for your marriage. If your marriage is not suffering from the attack of the enemy now, I encourage you to pray covering over your marriage before it does. If your marriage is under the attack of the enemy, then you must pray with double momentum. You must strategize your prayer with holy aggression. There are various forms of marital turbulence, but the truth is that the institution of marriage is under spiritual attack, and only the violent will take it by force.

Is your marriage suffering under the influence of evil powers? When a marriage is suffering from the evil powers of his father's house, you can easily identify such a marriage by its pattern. If your father-in-law was abusive to your mother-in-law, then it is likely that such a pattern could have found a way to place its traits on your husband. In the same manner, if your parents are divorced and you find your marriage experiencing almost the same kind of problems that led to your parent's divorce, it is likely that your marriage is suffering from the evil powers of your father's house.

Most marital turbulences today could be linked to infidelity. There are women out there who are comfortable having affairs with married men and vice versa. Some married women are classic prostitutes and have degrees in causing confusion in peoples' homes. Therefore, such women are called home wreckers or marriage breakers. They are dangerous and some of them use charms to keep their victims in perpetual bondage. That is why believers should not take anything to chance. Ask the Holy Spirit to reveal to you the root of your marital turbulence and guide you on how to effectively deliver your marriage from the forces that want to destroy it.

If you are a marriage breaker, as you read this book, I advise you to refrain from such practice and ask God to forgive you. I can attest to the changing and forgiving Power of God. The covenant of marriage should be honorable as ordained by God because any activity that brings dishonor to marriage will be met by the wrath of the righteous Judge above. The Scripture warns us in Hebrews 13:4: "Marriage *is* honorable among all, and the bed undefiled; but fornicators and adulterers God will judge." When the marital bed becomes defiled, trust is compromised, giving rise to diverse forms of marital turbulence.

A marriage could also suffer from the powers of household wickedness by the effect of polygamous marriages. Household wickedness can be a result of jealousy among the wives who use diabolic powers to affect the offspring of their rivalry wives. Some even go to the extent to make sure that the daughters of their rivalry wives do not get married and, if they do get married, that they end up in a divorce.

The issue behind the divorce might be very trivial, but because there is a stronghold warring against their destiny, divorce becomes inevitable. In such a family, you can see that either all the daughters are single and passed the right age of marriage or have returned home due to divorce. The reason could also be a result of an evil covenant. You must learn to pray with holy aggression to break every evil power demanding for your marriage.

Marital turbulence can also occur due to being unequally yoked. The consequences of such action of unequal yoking can become unbearable making the divorce process inevitable. My pastor once told a story that was told to him by a husband. The husband complained to the pastor that every morning when his wife wakes up, she would tidy only her own side of the bed. Isn't that something?

I remember once a sister came to me and when I inquired of her husband, she opened up in bitterness and responded, "Sister Lizzy, indeed, my husband is a real devil incarnate." Love has fallen apart and the center can no longer hold, but the good news is that God in His own divine mercy will change her situation for good and yours, too.

You must pray and cry out to God for His divine intervention. Prayer has the divine power to mandate change even in a very hopeless situation. I love the Scripture in Luke 1:37: "For with God nothing will be impossible." God has the final say to your problems Are you willing to have Him rule over your marriage? If yes, then get connected to the Power of Solutions through the strategic prayer declarations, and pray with holy aggression.

Do not allow the enemy to write the final chapter of your marriage. You are a winner by the virtue of the finished work of the Cross. Abandon your marriage in the hands of the Almighty God because He is the Power of Solutions to all marital turbulence.

I can attest to the dynamic effect of prayer. There have been times when I had thought of closing the chapters of my marriage, and I strongly believe that same thought had applied to my husband, too. But the saving grace of the blood and the effectual fervent prayer of the righteous has given birth to an unprecedented breakthrough. If you are contemplating a divorce, I strongly encourage you to hold on a little longer while trusting God. He will surely frustrate the wicked enterprises of the enemy.

Get a Scripture and hold God to it. One good day, the Almighty God above will bring your case to his remembrance and fight your battle. The strange man or woman meddling against the peace of your home will be judged and destroyed by the righteous judge; therefore, I encourage you to hold on a little longer and trust God in the process. The Bible says that "for with God nothing will be impossible" (Luke 1:37). The Power of Solutions is against marital turbulence with great force; therefore, I encourage you to hold on as you stand trusting God by His word.

The power of prayer cannot be an understatement. I have seen dead situations come to life because someone dared to pray and trust God. There are situations that will prompt you to voice out holy cries unto God especially when you have to contend with the powers contending against your destiny. Marriage is the most attacked institution because the enemy knows that when he destabilizes a home, the children become vulnerable to destruction. Therefore, you must position yourself aggressively to protect your home and ward off any evil arrows of the enemy by invoking God Almighty who is the Power of Solutions.

Here are some preventive measures to keep your marriage intact:

1. Choose your friends—some so-called friends are marriage breakers in disguise.
2. Pray with your spouse every day.
3. Ask God for wisdom to deal with issues as they manifest.
4. Be very careful with whom you confide.
5. Spend time with each other; spend weekends and vacations together.
6. Be transparent to each other.
7. Take your issues to God in prayer.

Prayer Declarations

1. My Bible tells me that what God has joined together let no man separate. Therefore, you strange powers working against my marriage, collide with the Rock of Ages. In the name of Jesus, I pray.

2. According to the ordinances of the word of God, I command every marital storm to be still in the name of Jesus.

3. Power of Solutions, manifest in my marriage, and destroy any home wrecker causing asunder in my home. In the name of Jesus, I pray.

4. Wicked women and men inside my marriage, are you still there? What are you doing there? I command you in the name of your Jesus, you will not destroy my home! Therefore, jump out of my marriage and destroy yourself in the mighty name of Jesus.

5. Home wreckers of my marriage, in the name of Jesus receive double disgrace and destruction.

6. My marriage you will not suffer in the hands of evil women and men, in the name of Jesus.

7. I will not mortgage my marriage in the bank of an adulterous woman, in the name of Jesus.

8. I will not mortgage my marriage in laps of fornicators, in the name of Jesus.

9. Evil powers of my father's house, boasting to destroy my home: you must die, in the name of Jesus.

10. Evil covenant, holding my marriage to ransom, break your hold, in the name of Jesus.

11. Evil altars making enchantment and divination over my marriage and my spouse, catch fire in the name of Jesus.

12. Garment of marital turbulence, catch fire in the name of Jesus.

13. Garment of marital disgrace, catch fire in the name of Jesus.

14. Garment of marital scandal, catch fire in the name of Jesus, I pray.

15. Power of divine Solutions, by the power of your word, manifest in my marriage and deliver my marriage. In the name of Jesus, I pray. AMEN.

Power of Solutions against Barrenness

Barrenness can occur in various areas of life: physical, economical, spiritual, and even geographical in nature.

Physical (physiological) Barrenness is an issue of infertility. An individual or an animal is unable to reproduce.

Economical Barrenness occurs when a financial institution is unable to make a profit or when a person's business stops yielding profit.

Spiritual Barrenness occurs when an individual or a church body is spiritually dead. When the presence of God is no longer felt and the zeal to pray or read the Bible is dry, it's an indication that the fire of God is needed to re-kind lives. Compromise is a senior brother to spiritual barrenness.

Geographical Barrenness occurs when the land or a specific geographical location is under a severe attack of famine. When a land is barren, the ability to yield its increase will fail. When a sea or river is barren, it will also refuse to yield its increase and the number of its creatures will diminish resulting in a limited catch.

The Bible gives an account where the land became barren for three consecutive years, so King David inquired of the Lord the reason for such occurrence. The Lord revealed that it was because of an action carried out by King Saul. Saul in his zeal had broken a covenant that his forefather had entered with the Gibeonites. Therefore, the land became cursed and went into rebellion resulting in a famine. The land refused to yield its increase and the people suffered. Restitution had to be made to the Gibeonites in order to arrest the power of famine that was holding the land in ransom.

Bareness could also be seen in the area of a business. When a business is no longer making profit or no longer productive it could be a result of bareness. It is always good to understand the underlying reason leading to the barren situation of the business. You want to know what the nature of the business is and if the activities occurring in the business are genuine and truthful. You want to know if the source of the initial set up fee was truthfully obtained or if it was from a stolen source. You want to know if the owner pays his or her tithe from his business profit especially if the business is Christian-based.

When a certain geographical location is heavily involved in atrocity, ninety percent of the time, the locality will experience some degree of barrenness. The land may decide to rebel and the result is evident as livestock become extinct and rivers seem to dry up. I once watched a video clip of a geographical location whose residents were highly involved in such sinful activities as incest, drugs, alcoholism, and more. As a result of their actions, the land rebelled and refused to yield its increase. Even the rivers almost dried up. However, when the few saints in the land cried out to God in repentance of the sins of the land, God heard their cry and revival broke out. The land was delivered and the people set free from the power of bondage. A great move of God was experienced as life sprung forth and the land indeed was healed. The people experienced unprecedented transformation. The land and the rivers came to life and started to bring forth their increase. Healing became inevitable because God is the Power of Solution against barrenness.

When the womb of a woman is not able to conceive, it could be considered barren. Barrenness could occur in the life of a woman due to several reasons. It could be due to a medical problem or it could be spiritual, which was the case when God closed the womb of Rachel. "When the Lord saw that Leah *was* unloved, He opened her womb, but Rachel *was* barren" (Genesis 29:31).

A barren situation prompted by the Hands of the Almighty God will need nothing short of His divine intervention. When God remembers your case, your affliction will automatically become history because the Power of Solutions has taken over your case. Hannah experienced the Power of Solutions over her barren situation. She was no longer comfortable with the love being showered to her by her beloved husband Elkanah. She knew that something greater was missing in her life; therefore, she arrived at her crossroad of decision. The decision, I believe, was either to continue her annual trip to Shiloh and get the biggest portion of meat or to rise up against the odds and seek the face of God in order to experience His divine touch. Thank goodness that Hannah decided to settle with the later. She took her case to the Power of Solutions and poured out her mind unto Him. God heard and answered her prayer and she brought forth a prophet in Israel—Samuel who was able to hear the very heartbeat of God. **"He grants the barren woman a home, like a joyful mother of children." (Psalm 113:9).**

Your season of victory is here. Therefore, by faith I declare that every barren situation in your life must receive divine transformation from the Power of Solutions and in the mighty name of Jesus, I pray this to be so. Amen.

Prayer Declarations

1. My Lord and my God, in the name of Jesus, heal our land.
2. Strongholds of my father's land that are preventing the land from yielding its increase, die in the name of Jesus.
3. Financial barrenness over my business, break your hold in the name of Jesus.
4. Avenues of wasted effort, close up in the name of Jesus.
5. Any power assigned to afflict my finances, die in the name of Jesus.
6. Let the power that resurrected Christ resurrect my womb, in the name of Jesus.
7. I convert my trials to testimonies, in the name of Jesus.
8. God of Hannah is my God; therefore, my story must change for good in the name of Jesus.
9. The God who remembered Sarah of my Bible, in the name of Jesus will remember me. I pray.
10. The God who remembered Leah of my Bible, in the name of Jesus, will remember me. I pray.
11. The God who remembered Hannah of my Bible, please remember me. In the mighty name of Jesus, I pray.
12. According to my Bible, the undisputable word of God, Mark 11.24 says that I can believe that my request has been answered, and I can claim it by faith in Jesus Christ. Amen.

Power of Solutions against Financial Poverty

*Beloved, I pray that you may prosper in all things and be
in health, just as your soul prospers.*

—3 John 2

It is the will of God that you prosper in all things: marriage, work, ministry, body, social life, finances, spirit—everything. Any department in your life experiencing less than God's blessing should not be accepted. Therefore, you must follow God's given protocol to wealthy living in order for him to unleash His uncommon blessings upon your life. Poverty is the opposite of prosperity. Therefore, you must reject it with all your might. You have to fight against laziness. Hard workers will have plenty of bread (see Proverbs 28:19). Do not be an infidel. Faith must accompany work. God has given us the power to get wealth. Go in the power of His word in whatever business you set your mind to perform.

There are rules that govern God's mandate for financial prosperity. When these rules are not met, it will create an avenue for the power of financial poverty to invade your financial domain. Here are some of the rules:

1. Pay your tithe (see Malachi 3:8-11).
2. Cultivate the habit of giving.
3. Sow a seed of faith and always name your seeds.
4. Believe that God is your source of provision, your Jehovah Jireh.
5. Put your faith to action. God does not believe in laziness. You must work to eat.
6. Do not covet falsely things that do not belong to you.
7. Do not steal to be rich.
8. Do not kill in order to possess the wealth of your victim, like unto Jezebel and Ahab.
9. Do not visit evil altars to assist you in acquiring wealth.
10. Do not gamble for wealth; the Bible calls that covetousness.
11. Learn to sow into the life of others; be a giver.
12. Do not restrain God's hand of blessings upon your life. Because if you do, it means you are inviting the power of poverty into your life. The wicked might become wealthy in their wickedness, but the day of God's judgment shall come and it will not be fun for them.

Genuine wealth comes from God. He gives the power to get wealth. He reveals divine business strategies to His people. God honors honorable business transactions by His people. His blessings add no sorrow.

There are also some foundational strongholds that could work against a believer's financial breakthrough. Evil foundations of wealth could be a factor. For example, if the business was inherited and the previous owner of the business had laid the foundation of the business on an evil ground, that could affect the progress of the business. What do I mean? Take, for instance, if the owner of the business had obtained the wealth falsely, and the business is now yours. As a child of God, the enemy will rise up to attack your business because the foundation of the business is faulty. That is why you have to plead the blood of Jesus and confess the sin of the previous owner of the business and anything you have in your possession as per means of inheritance. If the original owner of the business was not a born-again believer, the devil will not bother him or her because the devil already got such a person in bondage.

Some items you buy and keep in your office could also affect the growth of your business. Some individual working for you could also become your source of financial dilemma. That is why you must pray and seek the face of God to know who to hire and not hire.

Close every avenue the enemy might use to attack your finances. Trust God for any financial investment you wish to make. God is faithful, and the Holy Spirit will guide you aright. You will be like a tree planted by the rivers of water whose leaves are constantly green and fresh. This means God will continually be your supplier.

You cannot out-give God. Sow into peoples' lives. Sow into God's work, and sit down and watch him open the window of heaven for you as He blesses you beyond your wildest imagination. You will be satisfied even in times of famine because you are serving the creature of the heavens and the earth that has the power to command things in His will.

Prayer Declarations

1. Thank you Lord for you are my divine provider, in the name of Jesus.

2. I confess any crack in the foundation of my business and plead the blood of Jesus, I pray.

3. Strongholds of poverty, break your grip upon my finances, in the name of Jesus.

4. Evil foundation of my inherited business, receive the blood of Jesus and be cleansed, in the name of Jesus.

5. Any power and personality holding the progress of my business, release it now and die in the name of Jesus.

6. Witchcraft powers summoning my business to an evil court, in the name of Jesus scatter by fire.

7. Any evil money circulating in my bank account, be destroyed by the blood of Jesus.

8. Evil eyes monitoring my business transactions, receive blindness in the name of Jesus.

9. God of divine intervention, do something spectacular in my business and finances, I pray in the name of Jesus.

10. Uncommon favor, locate my business in the name Jesus.

11. Spirit of financial poverty in my life, I bind you in the name of Jesus. I pray.

12. I speak life to any dormant seed in my life, in the name of Jesus

13. Uncommon doors of financial blessings, open for me in the name of Jesus. I pray Amen.

14. Whether the devil likes it or not, money must go on errands for me in the name of Jesus to accomplish the work of the Lord.

15. In the Mighty name of Jesus, I am financially relevant.

The Power of Solutions to your problem is God Almighty Himself. Through the blood of Jesus, you are able to receive divine access to the power of Solutions for your breakthroughs. No matter how high the mountain stands before you, No matter how hopeless your situation might be, the truth is that when that situation is confronted by the Power of Solutions, a positive change must occur to favor you. **"For with God nothing will be impossible" (Luke 1:37)**.

Power of Solutions against Premature Death

I shall not die but live.
—Psalm 118:17

The will of God for us is that we enjoy life and faithfully serve Him. However, the enemy is geared at causing affliction on the children of God. The devil looks for any open door to strike at God's children. His visitation is three dimensional and very disastrous in nature. "The thief does not come except to steal, to kill, and to destroy. I have come that they may have life, and that they may have it more abundantly" (John 10:10).

God wants us to enjoy life more abundantly. Good health is included in the package as one of the benefits of salvation because He heals all your diseases and redeems your life from destruction. However, there are forces contending against your life. There are forces on assignment to terminate your life prematurely. There are forces embarking on making sure that they harvest your destiny. That is why you must not permit that to happen. You must fight with holy aggression in the name of Jesus through the power of prayer to obtain unprecedented breakthrough over the enemy of your life. You cannot afford to be a failure in the school of prayer because if you are, the enemy is bound to succeed; therefore, do not allow that to happen. I repeat, *do not allow the enemy to succeed in the affairs of your life.*

When the enemy comes like a flood, remember that the spirit of the Living God will always lift up a standard against Him because God is the Power of Solutions against the power contending against your life. Permit the Power of Solutions to manifest in your life by using His word. God honors His word above His name; therefore, when the enemy strikes you with his wicked arrows of affliction, all you have to do is use God's word against the enemy and return his wicked arrows back to him. When the enemy whispers death into your mind, say No! to the devil. Say, "I shall not die, but live, and declare the works of the Lord" (Psalm 118:17). Tell him that by the stripes of Jesus, you are healed. Command any evil deposit into your body to be uprooted and to return to its sender as Jesus did when He said, "Every plant which My heavenly Father has not planted will be uprooted" (Matthew 15:13).

Powers of premature death do not only come through bodily afflictions. They come in various dimension as earlier indicated. They come through physical enemies and through demonic instigation like unto Haman who dug a gallow for Mordecai for a premature death; but thanks be to God, who was on his side. Therefore, Haman became the very recipient of his own wicked enterprise (see the Book of Esther). Any power or personality demanding your life on a platter must die in your place.

Premature death could manifest through accident as unto the powers of bloodsucking demons on highways and byways by pre-empting or masterminding accidents. Sometimes, accidental deaths might occur as a result of sheer negligence. It could occur as a result of disobedience unto God, which sometimes would cause God's protection over the individual to lift. That's why it's very important that you run to God, and ask for His forgiveness whenever you fail. Don't give the enemy any room to invade your life because it could be very dangerous.

According to Ecclesiastes 10:8: "He who digs a pit will fall into it, and whoever breaks through a wall will be bitten by a serpent." Therefore, I advise you to be spiritually vigilant and maintain an offensive position while protecting your spiritual wall from cracking. Sin is the primary cause for a wall to crumble. You must possess the gate of your invisible enemy by calling unto God the Power of Solutions who has the final verdict for your life through Christ Jesus and by His word in Jeremiah 29:11, which says, "For I know the thoughts that I think toward you, says the Lord, thoughts of peace and not of evil, to give you a future and a hope." Therefore, you are a winner in Jesus and your future is sure in Him.

I once heard a preacher say that the graveyard is the wealthiest place on earth because there lie the remains of great men and women with untapped skills and wisdom. Yet, some might be a result of the power of premature death and destiny killers. You must tell the devil in very clear terms that your life will not be harvested prematurely by any wicked power in the name of Christ Jesus. You must know the truth, and the truth will make you free. The Bible states that life is in the blood and the blood of Jesus is your ransom; therefore, you are untouchable, unreachable, and invisible to the powers of wickedness. The blood of Jesus is also your shield of defense warding off any evil arrow fired toward your life. The Power of Solution—Jesus Himself—has taken away the sting of death, and death has been swallowed up in victory. Praise the Lord!

You must learn to confess life and not death. You must learn to walk daily in divine health. You must let the devil know that you are cognizant of your divine authority to declare life even in the presence of what looks like death. Your life is not for sale, so magnify God with it as you connect to the Power of Solutions for your life sustaining divine vitality.

Prayer Declarations

1. In the name of Jesus, I shall not die but live to declare the works of God.
2. Any power contending to harvest my life prematurely, in the name of Jesus, you will not succeed.
3. I destroy any wicked embargo upon my life, in the name of Jesus.
4. Powers of death, I command you to destroy yourselves, in the name of Jesus.
5. I shall fulfill my destiny by the grace and mercy of God. I pray.
6. Any power demanding for my head on a platter, you will not succeed in the name of Jesus.
7. My life is hidden in Christ, in God; therefore, my protection is sure in the name of Jesus.
8. I will declare the goodness of God upon my life, in the His vineyard. I pray.

9. I frustrate every conspiracy against my life, in the name of Jesus.

10. My life will not be mortgaged in the hands of my enemy; I pray in Jesus' name.

11. I declare my life untouchable, invisible, and unreachable to the powers of wickedness.

12. My Lord and My God, manifest yourself as the Power of Solutions against the powers of death. In the name of Jesus, I pray Amen.

God is the Power of Solutions over your life and over the problems challenging the peace of your life. Therefore, you must learn to release all that concerns you into His Mighty hands. God is faithful as He watches over His words to perform that which He has spoken concerning you. God cannot fail. The power of death cannot rule over your life. Death has been swallowed up in victory; therefore, we have life abundantly in Christ Jesus. And in His name we have total victory over all the evil forces coming against us.

Power of Solutions is speaking in your favor. God is fighting all your visible and invisible battles because you are a winner in Christ Jesus; therefore, shout Hallelujah! Amen.

POWER OF SOLUTIONS AGAINST "TITLE SYNDROME"

The church is getting entangled in what I call the "title syndrome." Almost everybody wants to be called a Bishop, Apostle, General Overseer, Pastor, Evangelist, Prophet, Doctor, Reverend, etc. There is no problem with having a title per se. However, it becomes a problem when people become so entangled in their title syndrome and self-exaltation that they fail to realize when the anointing of God has lifted. King Saul was so busy chasing shadows, he didn't even realize that his throne had been taken away from him and his kingship anointing had lifted. Sad indeed!

Eli was in a state of complacency and did not realize that the glory of God had departed from him and from the land. However, his daughter-in-law was spiritual enough to recognize this fact. The overwhelming doom surrounding her led to the naming of her new-born child "Ichabod" meaning "God's glory has departed."

By doing so, she was confirming that the glory of God indeed had departed from the land as God's judgment was evident.

Saul was very infatuated with his kingship title, for he bluntly refused to acknowledge that his kingship anointing has been transferred to David. He wanted to hold onto that title so desperately to the extent of eliminating whoever stood in his way. Unfortunately for him, God's mind was made up. David was chosen and the will of God prevailed.

You can't cry over spilled milk. Therefore, try not to spill your milk. The problem today is that people get so entangled with titles and forget the rules guiding the title behind their names. When one gets caught up in the title syndrome in the church, a person feels that he or she has "arrived" and spends less time fasting and studying the word of God. When a servant of God is up there on the pedestal of spiritual elevation and feels that he or she does not need God for directions or is beyond temptation, beloved, know that such a person is a candidate of an inevitable crashing fall.

I am not looking for a church where Bishop John or Apostle Peter is the leader. I am looking for a church where the presence of God is in charge because wherever God is "signs and wonders" will follow. Do not go to a church seeking after the man of God. I encourage you to seek God who is the miracle worker himself. If you are in a church because of Bishop Tim or Apostle Ben, when they fail, you will be highly disappointed. But if you are there because of God, then when the storm of life strikes in your local assembly, you will be spiritually strong enough to pray for the man of God. That is why you cannot put your trust in the "arm of flesh" for there is a possibility for them to fail you because they are operating within the arena of flesh and blood. In essence, they are human beings with the tendency to falter. However, I come with the good tiding that God never fails. In Him is Yea and in Him is Amen. His Words remain infallible.

The greatest title holder is the king of kings, the Lord of lords, the Alpha and the Omega, the beginning and the end, the Prince of peace, the Counselor, the greatest Physician, the greatest Intercessor, our Strong Tower, etc! etc! And in it all, Jesus remains the gentle Shepherd and Servant for us to emulate as the measuring yardstick to the walk of the High Calling.

Brother and Apostle Paul being cognizant of the power of the flesh and the danger of the "I have arrived title syndrome," kept himself in constant check of his spiritual tempo. He made up his mind and focused on the finishing line of the high calling.

Men and women can easily get derailed as they become affluent or as their ministry becomes bigger in size; they want to take the glory that belongs to God. That is a dangerous position, so it's important that we perform periodic spiritual checks or inventory on ourselves to know if we are still standing and make amends where necessary. Remember that we are still in the embodiment of flesh and blood and there is no human being born on earth who is beyond temptation. Paul declares, "I do not run like someone running aimlessly; I do not fight like a boxer beating the air. No, I strike a blow to my body and make it my slave so that after I have preached to others, I myself will not be disqualified for the prize" (1 Corinthians 9:26-27).

It would be wonderful if the body of Christ becomes more interested in things that download the presence of the Holy Spirit in the church, such as the fruits of the spirit rather than entangling themselves in the title syndrome. While the afflicted are getting worse, the fornicators, adulterers, thieves, liars, murderers, witches, and wizards are waxing stronger in the house of God. The anointing of God is no longer present in the house of God to convict, to break yokes, and to set the captives free. The church is under siege and desperately in need of deliverance from the top to the bottom.

I was told of a story where a church had invited a mighty man of God as their guest speaker for an upcoming crusade. The host church, while preparing for the Crusade, had embarked on prayer and fasting also committing the man of God to prayer. However, while the host pastor was praying, he had a word from the Lord for the man of God. The Lord said to him, "When the man of God arrives, ask him, 'When was the last time you slept with a woman that is not your wife?'" The host pastor was taken aback by such an assignment. However, he had to do what the Lord had asked him to do.

When the host pastor picked up the man of God from the airport, he took him to his church office where the spirit of God came over him again prompting him to ask the man of God the question. The host pastor was somewhat uncomfortable, but he told the guest pastor, "While praying for you and for the crusade, the Lord told me to ask you a question." The host pastor continued, "Man of God." He said. "God wants me to ask you this question: 'When was the last time you had sex with a woman who is not your wife?'" To his great surprise, the guest pastor responded, knowing that it was God who wanted to expose him.

He answered, "Last night."

That was a man of God with a title and, yet, he was still suffering from the power of the flesh—a destroying force against the men and women of the cloth. That's why we must be cognizant of the fact that the enemy is not perturbed by your title. The enemy is busy and cares less if you are a Bishop, Apostle, Father, Knight, Arch Bishop, Pastor, Teacher, Deacon, Deaconess, Elder, Rev. Dr. G.O. etc! etc! if you give him a bite, he will take a mouthful; therefore, watch and pray as you break the yoke of the title syndrome. Yearn for greater heights and uncommon anointing that would demonstrate the awesome power of the almighty Jehovah in your life and in the lives of the members of your congregation in the name of Jesus as you plug into the socket of the Power of Solutions. Stop the enemy before he stops you.

Man and woman of God, do recognize your purpose and be driven by it because a purpose-driven life will surely fulfill your destiny by the grace and mercy of God. Remember that you are a winner through the finished work of the cross, so utilize the authority you have over the enemy to your advantage. Do not get derailed by title this and title that. If you have all those titles by your name and no anointing to defend it, the devil will look at you and laugh and toss you like a football in his hand because he knows you are not a threat. "So then it is not of him who wills, nor of him who runs, but of God who shows mercy" (Romans 9:16).

God's mercy cannot be an overstatement as you embark on this glorious race for a glorious prize of a glorious crown for the glorious people who have been redeemed by the glorious blood of Jesus Christ—the final order. I declare in the name of Jesus that by the grace of God, you will make it to the finishing line and will then receive the most awaited words: "Well done thou faithful servant" from the Master Himself, Jesus, as He decorates you with the most befitting title of accomplishment of the race to abundance of life.

Prayer Declarations

1. I break the yoke of title syndrome in my life, in the name of Jesus.
2. Any wicked power in the heavenlies lying in wait in order to pull me down, be disappointed in the name of Jesus.

3. In the name of Jesus, I frustrate any wicked hand assigned to turn the clock of my calling backward.

4. My head, you will not carry the yoke of shame in the mighty name of Jesus.

5. Evil load of pride, I drop you in the name of Jesus

6. Evil load of "I have arrived syndrome," I drop you in the name of Jesus.

7. Any power assigned to make me miss the mark of my high calling in Christ Jesus, I frustrate you in the name of Jesus.

8. I humble myself under the cross, in the name of Jesus.

9. I put on the garment of the fruits of the spirit, in the name of Jesus.

10. My Lord and my God, demonstrate your power in my life. In the mighty name of Jesus, I pray. Amen.

11. Anointing to win souls for the kingdom of God, baptize my life in the name of Jesus.

POWER OF SOLUTIONS AGAINST OUR CHILDREN'S DESTINY KILLERS

Here am I and the children whom the LORD has given
me, we are for signs and wonders in Israel from the
LORD of Host who dwells in Mount Zion.
—Isaiah 8:18

Children are always a replacement of their parent's future generation. That is why it is very important for parents to speak blessings into the lives of their children. Abraham pronounced blessings into the life of Isaac. Isaac also pronounced blessings into the lives of his sons. Jacob in Genesis 49 called up his sons and prophetically spoke into their lives. Parental blessings have a futuristic impact in the lives of your children which is also transferred into the lives of your grandchildren.

Children are a source of joy and blessings to the parents and, more importantly, they are a reward from God. "Behold, children are a heritage from the LORD, the fruit of the womb a reward. Like arrows in the hand of a warrior, so are the children of one's youth. Happy is the man who has his quiver full of them. They shall not be ashamed, but shall speak with their enemies in the gate" (Psalm 127:3-5).

The above Scripture reveals that children are a blessing and not a curse. They are a source of joy and dignity to their parents. They are the future generation of the parents. The devil is also cognizant of this fact; that is why he fights so hard to get to our children. His utmost desire is to cage and destroy their destiny. Therefore, parents, we must not allow the plans of the enemy to prevail. The sanctity of a Christian home is paramount to the bringing up of the children whom the Lord has given to us. We also know the devil is against the union of marriage and continues to fire arrows of destabilization that would create avenues to destroy children and their destiny. When the Shepherd (the parent) is arrested, the sheep will scatter.

As parents, we have our God-given assignment to train up our children in the way of the Lord. We have the obligation to tell our children the truth of life. We have the obligation to instill discipline in our children. We have the obligation to teach them the difference between good and evil because if we don't, someone else might tell them the opposite of the truth. We cannot afford not to pray for our children, especially in this present-day generation where the enemy has established so much distorted truth and morals in our younger ones.

Most television shows are now comfortable showing programs that are not normal for certain age groups to watch, and no one is complaining about it. There are talk shows with unbelievable characters appearing as guests. The enemy is really busy and having a ball as he tries so hard to line up the younger generation to hell. In schools and universities, a reversed lifestyle is not considered immoral because people are comfortable with it and call it "the right of choice." The enemy is a liar.

My Bible tells me that God created Adam and Eve and both became parents—that is the acceptable biblical foundation for a Christian home. The devil cannot argue this truth, and you must tell your children the truth based on biblical guidelines. As a parent, I encourage you to teach your children to search the Scriptures for themselves and continue to pray for them. The enemy will not stop going after your children. The days are very evil and the forces warring against them are coming from all directions; however, persistent prayer will prevail for your children because prayer is the mandate for divine intervention to occur. The children whom God has given you are for signs and wonders, indeed.

But young kids are locked up in jail for years because of crimes they have no business involving themselves with just because the enemy is busy in their lives. For such a reason, they spend most of their lives behind the jail walls resulting in an aborted destiny. I once had the privilege to walk into a state prison where a first, second, and third generation felons were all serving. My heart went out to them because the enemy had done that.

Sometimes the enemy gets to the children through indulging them in drunk driving and, in so doing, many lives have been wasted in their prime. Peer pressure is also one of the forces the enemy uses to get to our children. We, the parents, must pray with holy aggression against the attacks of the enemy over the lives of our children. We must teach our children the truth in the word of God. We must revisit their foundation with the blood of Jesus and plead the blood of Jesus while asking for forgiveness where we as parents have failed to effectively perform our divinely assigned duties.

Parents must learn to apply "tough love" with our children when necessary in order to impute a sense of discipline. When a child has no sense of discipline the consequences of their choices will always return for judgment. Therefore, an old adage that "parents must learn to chase after the black hen while the day is bright" applies.

Children must be told the truth—that it is not right to have a child out of wedlock. Unfortunately, the enemy has spiritually blinded most people of this generation and, at the same time, created a monstrous world where even some parents are comfortable seeing their daughters pregnant out of wedlock. Some have become sexually and morally deterred possessing reprobate minds while the devil sits behind and laughs knowing that his actions to enlarge hell seems to be gaining more ground.

Knowing that our children are our future generation, we must therefore protect their destiny with prayers that avail much, and do so in the name of Jesus. Samson was a child anointed from the womb, but the desire for a prostitute named Delilah cost him his destiny; therefore, he died prematurely. That will not be the lot of our children, in the name of Jesus. Amen.

The sons of Eli, Hophni, and Phinehas were also involved in sinful activities without remorse nor repentance, so the glory of God had to depart from the land, making room for the enemy to gain entrance. The covering of protection was lifted; they died in the battlefield prematurely because the enemies were after their lives instigating them not to adhere to the warnings. Our children will hear and adhere to the voice of God. This will not be the lot of our children in the name of Jesus.

Samson was ordained from his mother's womb a Nazarene. He was a child singled out by God Himself for great exploits. Has his destiny aborted as he entangled himself unequally with Delilah? It was his wife who plotted and executed his destruction. Samson's disobedience was the cause of his aborted destiny. He married the wrong wife. I pray that our children will not make marital choices of destruction in the mighty name of Jesus. Young man, young lady, listen to your parents because they sometimes are in the position to discern and advise based on wisdom. However, the utmost direction to follow is in the word of God and through prayer.

Protect and guard your destiny with trembling and fear. Sometimes some decisions have to be made and followed through with, such as friendship elimination, job elimination, or lifestyle changes. Anything that the Bible warns to abstain from are destructive to our souls and more often our body. Therefore, do not allow the enemy of disobedience to abort your destiny. Do not do hard drugs because it is an epitome of destiny destruction. Sex outside of marriage is also destructive. Therefore, leave it alone and stay focused with your education and the things of God. Children must honor their parents because it is the right thing to do, and it will result to longevity. This is my advice to young people, and I believe that I have the mind of God by His grace to tell you the truth.

Make the following prayer declarations with holy aggression, and recover your children if any are in the camp of the enemy.

Prayer Declarations

1. The children whom God has given me are for signs and wonders, in the mighty name of Jesus.
2. The enemy will not mortgage my children, in the name of Jesus.
3. I will not sorrow over my children, in the Mighty name of Jesus.

4. Any power assigned to abort the destiny of my children, you are a liar. In the name of Jesus, you will not succeed.

5. Bell of regret and disappointment, you will not jingle in the lives of my children, in the mighty name of Jesus.

6. Any power assigned to terminate the life of my children/ child you are a liar destroy yourself in the name of Jesus.

7. My children you will not be a candidate for jail in the mighty name of Jesus.

8. My children you will not partake in any perversed lifestyle in the name of Jesus.

9. Powers of peer pressure, I pressure you out of the lives of my children, in the name of Jesus.

10. My children, whether the devil likes it or not, you will serve my God and His name is Jehovah, in the mighty name of Jesus.

11. In the name of Jesus, I recover my children from the camp of the enemy.

12. I recover my children from the camp of failure, in the name of Jesus.

13. I recover my children from the camp of destiny terminators, in the name of Jesus.

14. I recover my children from the camp of runaway spirits, in the name of Jesus.

15. I recover my children from the camp of prostitution and pornography, in the name of Jesus.

16. I break every curse in the lives of my children, in the name of Jesus.

17. I break every evil yoke in their lives, in the name of Jesus.

18. Wasters of lives, hear me clearly, my children are not your candidates, in the mighty name of Jesus. Therefore, you will not waste their lives.

19. Drinkers of blood, my children are not your candidate, in the mighty name of Jesus.

20. Eaters of flesh, my children are not your candidates, in the mighty name of Jesus

21. Therefore, in the name of Jesus, you the enemy of my children's destiny, waste your own life, drink your own blood, and eat your own flesh.

22. My children, you are for signs and wonders, in the name of Jesus.

23. My Lord and My God, in the name of Jesus, do something spectacular in the lives of my children. I pray thee.

24. My Lord and My God, demonstrate your power in the lives of my children, in the mighty name of Jesus.

25. I will rejoice and glorify God over the lives of my children, in the name of Jesus I pray.

26. Blood of Jesus, visit the foundation of my children's lives and purge out every seed of wickedness planted into it. In the name of Jesus I pray.

27. I uproot every evil plant in the foundation of my children's lives, in the name of Jesus.

28. With the blood of Jesus, I erase every evil word spoken over the lives of my children, in the name of Jesus.

29. Fear of God, possess the lives of my children, in the name of Jesus.

30. I cover my children in the protective power of the blood of Jesus, and I declare them untouchable, unreachable, and invisible to the powers of wickedness from today. Henceforth, in the mighty name of Jesus, I pray. Amen.

POWER OF SOLUTIONS AGAINST LOSS

And now I urge you to take heart, for there will be no
loss of life among you, but only of the ship.
—Acts 27:22

The Bible talks about various kinds of loss—the lost sheep, the lost coin, the lost son, (see Luke 15), and the lost axe (see 2 Kings 6). These all have a loss in common. The lost sheep was found because the shepherd was a good one. The story of the lost coin indicates the fervency a woman will exhibit to recover her lost coin. The lost son, despite his wasteful life when he decided to return to his dad, the joy in his daddy's heart triggered a welcome banquet in his honor. As his dad declared that his lost son has been found. The lost axe was brought floating to the top of the river as God mandated the defilement of the law of gravity to honor the prophet of God because loss is not acceptable with God.

Have you gone away like a lost sheep? Have you lost the zeal of your salvation? Have you lost your wife or husband to a strange man or woman? Have you lost your kids to drugs and to a perverse lifestyle? Have you lost your zeal of praying and fasting? Have you lost the zeal to study your Bible or to attend church services? If so, I have good news for you. The truth is that there shall be no loss for the believers. You shall not suffer any loss, "for the Son of Man has come to seek and to save that which was lost" (Luke 19:10).

You have the divine authority in the word of God to recover any loss and to stop any impending loss in the name of Jesus. The most important loss is the loss of one's soul. The mandate from heaven was to reconcile man to God through the utmost sacrificial work of the cross. Christ paid that debt; therefore, there shall be no loss of soul. Every other loss is recoverable, but the loss of a soul is a gain in hell and God does not find pleasure in that; therefore, we are urged to work out our salvation with trembling and fear. You must position yourself to fight against any kind of loss. You will not lose your job. You will not lose your children. You will not lose the anointing upon your life, Your ministry will not suffer loss. Indeed, you will wax stronger in the things of the Lord. The enemy will not cause you to suffer any sort of loss by the grace and mercies of God.

There shall be no loss in your life, in the mighty name of Jesus.

Prayer Declarations

1. By the grace of God, I declare that I shall not suffer any loss in the name of Jesus.
2. Any power echoing loss into my life, I silence you forever.

3. I pursue, overtake, and recover all that the enemy has stolen from me, in the name of Jesus.

4. By the authority in the name of Jesus, I bind the spirit of loss in my life.

5. I bind the spirit of loss in my foundation, in the name of Jesus.

6. I bind the powers of loss warring against my spiritual and physical gain, in the name of Jesus.

7. Anything inside of me attracting the spirit of loss, jump out and die in the name of Jesus.

8. Any aura attracting loss into my life, blow away in the name of Jesus.

9. Arrows of loss fired into my life, backfire in the name of Jesus.

10. By the grace of God, I refuse to suffer any sort of loss, in the name of Jesus.

11. Spirit of loss hear me clearly, in the name of Jesus I reject you.

12. With the blood of Jesus, I protect myself and my family from any kind of loss. In the mighty name of Jesus. I pray.

POWER OF SOLUTIONS
AGAINST FAILURE

Failure is a terrible spirit. Failure is very handicapping. The spirit of failure must be overcome within the three dimensions of your very existence your spirit, soul, and body. It is a very negative force aimed to destroy its victim.

Failure will tell you, "You can't do it. Everybody has tried but did not succeed how then do you think you will?" Failure will paint pictures of discouragement in your mind to stop your efforts. Failure will enumerate reasons why you cannot succeed. Some of the reasons are:

1. Your parents were failures, so why do you think you can make it?
2. You don't have a "Godfather" to help you secure a job in such an establishment, so why even try.

3. You need a lot of money to start that sort of business, so just forget it.
4. This kind of profession will take you nowhere, so why go to school.
5. You have taken that exam so many times; so give up.
6. You can't afford to build a house now because the building materials are very expensive, so forget the idea.
7. I will start the project next year. That is procrastination—the thief of time.
8. Failure will show you mountains that you have to climb in order to get to the other side.
9. Failure will exhibit itself through fear and present roadblocks of discouragement.
10. Failure will come as a yoke of burden to keep you suppressed and incapacitate your zeal.

Understanding the power of failure will help you fight against it. Stand up against the dilapidating effect of failure by utilizing the word of God such as in Philippians 4:13, which says, "*I can do all things through Christ who strengthens me.*" Yes, you can do all things through Him whose word remains infallible and inerrant.

I know of a man who ran for the office of the president several times and failed. He refused to give up, and his persistency paid off. He eventually got the votes and became the president. Abraham Lincoln was his name. He knew the power of failure but refused to embrace it; instead, he decided to embrace the will to succeed. You can only be a failure when you stop to try. Therefore, stay focused and your persistence will eventually pay off. God cannot fail because that is not his nature. His promises are sure and amen.

David was an epitome of success. He did not allow himself to be intimidated by the gruesome height of Mr. Goliath. He knew what success meant, and he embraced it wholeheartedly with the mindset of the capabilities of his God. You must know your God. His plan for your life is to see you succeed. **"For I know the thoughts that I think toward you, says the Lord, thoughts of peace and not of evil, to give you a future and a hope" (Jeremiah 29:11).**

With such assurance, it is now left to you to embrace it and flow with the blessing. You are made for great exploits. You have the blueprint of God to succeed. Failure should not be found any way near to your domain. You are surrounded by a great cloud of success. The river of success flows through you. I want to stir up the spirit to succeed that is already in you. Your spirit, soul, and body must collaborate with the spirit of success. No matter the degree of failure you have encountered in life, I come to tell you today that the blood of Jesus has a better covenant with you, and it is the covenant of success in the mighty name of Jesus.

Remember Jabez, who was sick and tired of his situation. He knew he could do better than what his life was experiencing, so he cried out to God to change his situation. God heard him and granted his request. God will hear your cry today, and your situation will change for good. Pray these prayer points with holy aggression. Give that perpetual liar a mandate for eviction from your mind because you now have a renewed mind. You have the mind of God.

Prayer Declarations

1. In the name of Jesus, I command the spirit of failure in my life to die now.
2. I uproot every evil plant of failure in my life, in the name of Jesus.
3. I plant the seed of success into my foundation, and I water it with the blood of Jesus.
4. With the blood of Jesus, I erase every word of failure written in my life.
5. From today, I put on the garment of success, in the mighty name of Jesus.
6. Spirit of failure, I reject you, in the mighty name of Jesus.
7. I command the clouds of failure hovering over my life to roll away now, in the name of Jesus.
8. I command every garment of failure in my life to catch fire, in the name of Jesus.
9. By the special grace of God, my life will succeed.
10. By the special grace of God, my business will succeed.
11. By the special grace of God, my family will succeed.
12. By the special grace of God, my marriage will succeed.
13. By the special grace of God, my children will succeed.
14. By the special grace of God, my wife/husband will succeed.
15. By the special grace of God, my career will succeed.
16. By the special grace of God, my ministry will succeed.
17. By the special grace of God, my parents will succeed.
18. By the special grace of God, my siblings will succeed.
19. By the special grace of God, my bank account will experience success.

20. By the special grace of God, from today success will know my name.

21. By the special grace of God, money will go on errands for me.

22. By the special grace of God, Christ will be glorified in my success.

23. By the special grace of God, I will control my wealth, and my wealth will not control me.

24. By the special grace of God, my success will not add any sorrow to my life.

25. By the special grace of God, I have become a financier for the gospel of our Lord and Savior Jesus Christ.

Beloved, you are born to succeed. You have Jesus on your side; therefore, success from now onward will know your name. My prayer is that as you swim in the river of success, your love for Jesus will not wax cold. I pray that God will be glorified in all your ways and you will not forget to acknowledge that He is the one who gives you the power to get wealth. I pray that you will not become too successful to forget Him who has blessed you abundantly. I pray that you will not become too successful to the extent to compromise your faith. I pray that you will not be too successful to lose the joy of your salvation. I pray that any of the possible errors mentioned above will not be your portion by the special grace of God. **"For what profit is it to a man if he gains the whole world, and loses his own soul?" (Matthew 16:26).**

Think on this Scripture as you enjoy the blessings of the Lord that makes rich and add no sorrow. God will bless you beyond your wildest imagination. Keep your faith alive.

How to Receive Jesus

*If you confess with your mouth the Lord Jesus and
believe in your heart that God has raised Him from the
dead, you will be saved. For with the heart one believes
unto righteousness, and with the mouth confession is
made unto salvation.*
—Roman 10: 9-10.

The process of receiving Jesus into your life must be voluntary. You must not be forced to make this confession. It must spring out of a personal conviction to commit. The truth is that God is faithful to His word. Heaven and Hell are real. The decision to go to either one will be solely yours to make. I pray you will choose to go to heaven where Jesus will reign forever with all those who believe in Him.

God bless you and congratulations on receiving Him as your personal Savior.

BOOKS BY THE AUTHOR

- ➤ **The Dynamics of a Breakthrough Prayer**
- ➤ **Like unto an Intercessor**
- ➤ **How to Identify and Destroy Evil Patterns in Your Life: Spiritual Warfare Revealed**
- ➤ **Not Beyond Struggles: Pastors Also Cry**
- ➤ **Prayer MapQuest: A Prayer Handbook for Prayer Radicals**